Most of the dogs were shy and stayed in the shadows, but two little scruffballs, their noses twitching, bravely came forward.

They gobbled up the meat and cheekily looked up as if to ask for more! The man, who was called Oleg, smiled. He knew at once he had found what he was looking for.

Oleg

Oleg was a scientist at Moscow's Space Centre and was hoping to find two special dogs who might be brave enough for a very important mission.

The two new arrivals were named Belka and Strelka. They were given a tasty dinner and a kennel of their own.

For the first time in their lives they had enough to eat and a warm place to sleep.

There were dogs of every kind at the Centre: some were bold and playful, some were snappy or growly, some were gentle and well-behaved. But Belka and Strelka stood out. They were clever and calm, brave and obedient. Oleg was delighted!

All the dogs were given a health check, then weighed and measured to make sure they weren't too big or too small for the mission. Belka and Strelka were just the right size!

eyes

ears

teeth

heart

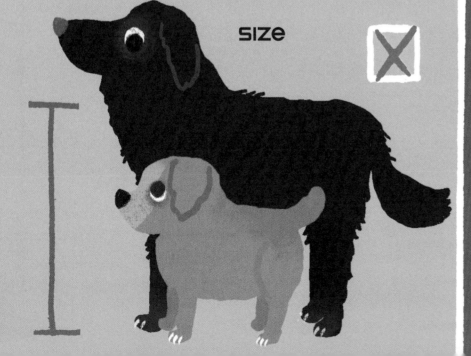

size

weight

After all the tests were complete, Oleg had
to decide which two dogs would be chosen.

Finally, he made up his mind.

He gathered the dogs together
to make his announcement.

The two brave little strays he had found on the streets were soon to become the most famous dogs in the world!

Belka and Strelka
were going to be…

Belka and Strelka were going on a special mission to space, to fly all the way around the Earth – a journey called an orbit. They seemed to know something exciting was happening. They wagged their tails; they were ready to start training straight away.

The two little cosmonauts needed to get used to how it would feel inside the rocket. Some of the exercises were:

Practising staying calm with loud noises around them;

spending time in special kennels to get used to being on their own away from people;

WOOOOF!

and standing on a platform that shook under their paws.

They practised again and again, until they were finally ready for their mission. There was only one thing left to do: put on their special doggy spacesuits – a red one for Strelka and a green one for Belka.

LAUNCH DAY
19 AUGUST 1960

Finally, the big day arrived. The rocket stood on the launch pad ready for blast-off. Belka and Strelka were ready too.

The rocket shuddered, shook, rumbled and roared...

then broke free and soared into the sky!

Up and up it went through the clouds until it reached space. Belka and Strelka's great adventure had begun!

All was still
and quiet as
Belka and Strelka
began their orbit.

The ground crew watched on their television monitors. Everything was working as it should. But why were Belka and Strelka so still?

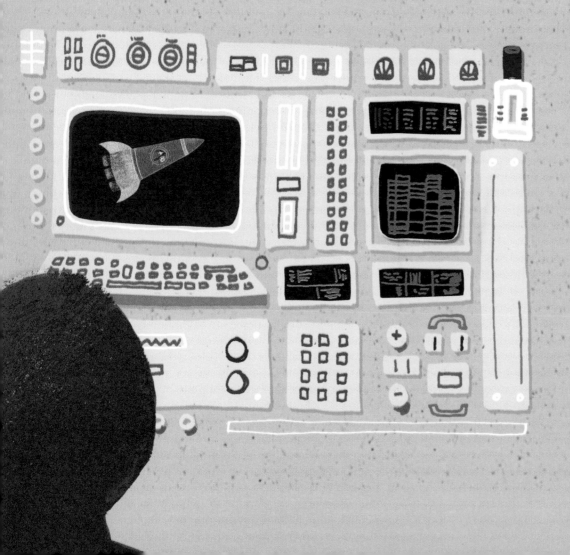

Everyone held their breath.

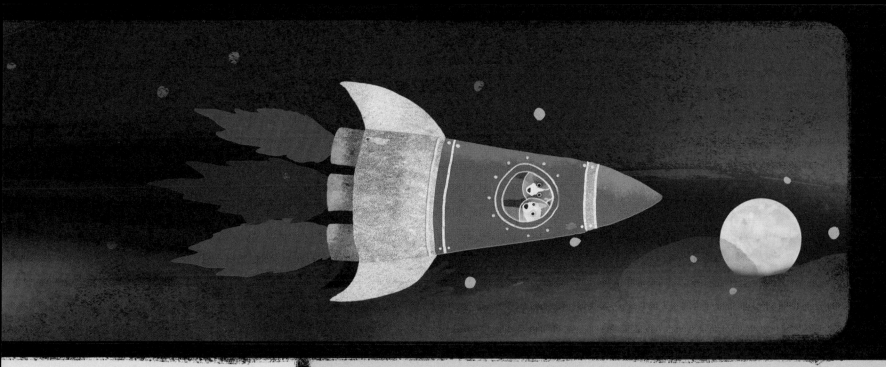

Belka and Strelka were not moving *at all*.

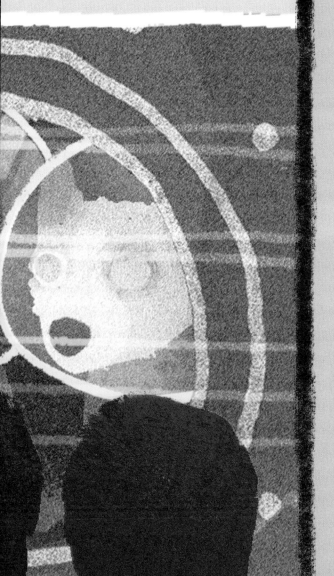

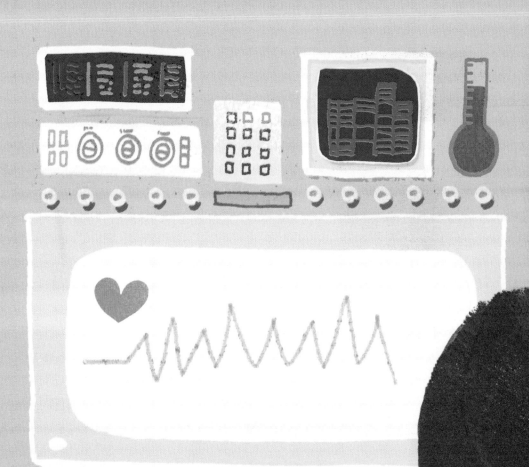

Minutes turned into hours. It was feared the brave little space dogs had not survived the launch.

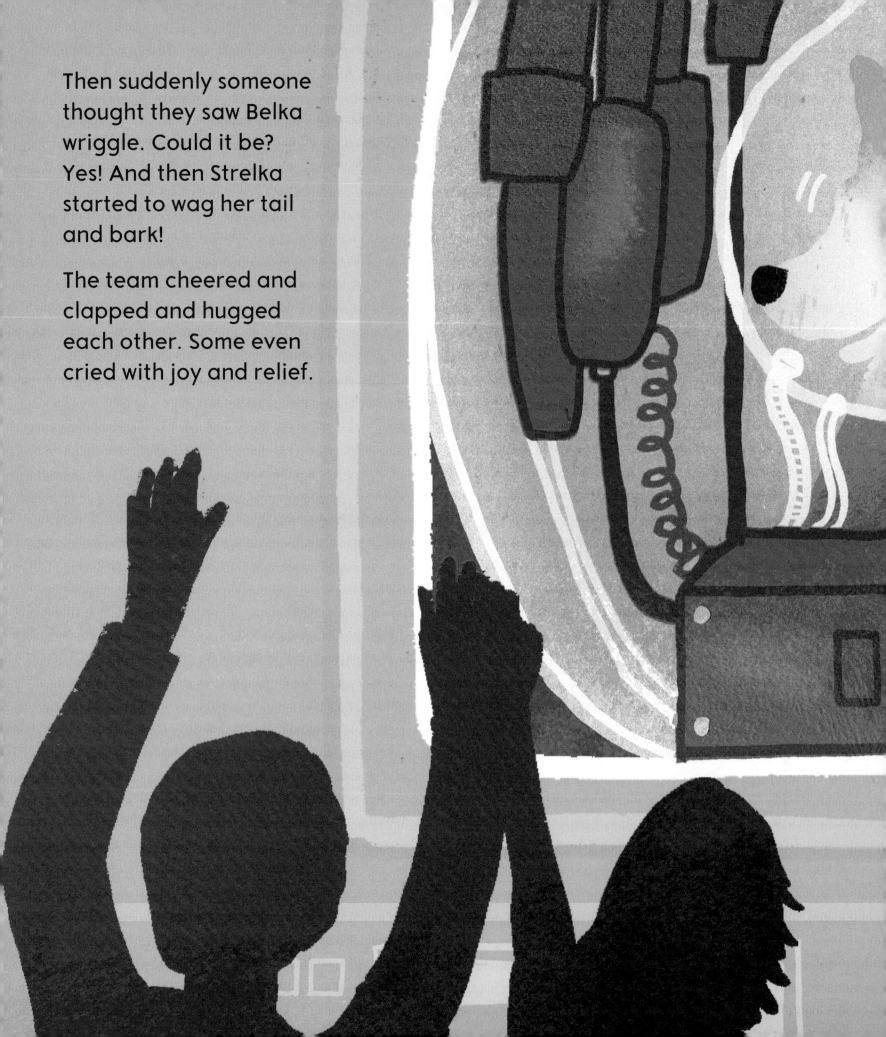

Then suddenly someone thought they saw Belka wriggle. Could it be? Yes! And then Strelka started to wag her tail and bark!

The team cheered and clapped and hugged each other. Some even cried with joy and relief.

Belka and Strelka were

ALIVE!

Round and round the Earth they flew. They saw the blue of the oceans and the greens and browns of the land shining against the blackness of space. Not even a human had seen such sights!

Belka and Strelka circled the
Earth many times until, at last,
it was time to go home.

As the spacecraft zoomed back into Earth's atmosphere, flames began to lick at the windows.

Down, down they plummeted at high speed.
The team at the space station grew very quiet.
Landings could be dangerous.

Then suddenly, a parachute opened and slowed the spacecraft down. Belka and Strelka watched the ground getting closer and closer ...

...and closer.

The rescue team was waiting.

THUMP!

They rushed to the spacecraft and flung open the door. Two little faces peeped out. Two little tails started wagging. And two brave little dogs were gently lifted out safe and well. Belka and Strelka were home.

Within a few hours of landing, news of Belka and Strelka's amazing journey had spread all around the world. They were celebrated and loved everywhere they went.

Pictures of them appeared everywhere – on stamps and postcards, on television and in newspapers. Even films and cartoons were made about their adventures.

Everyone wanted to see the two brave little dogs that had flown around the Earth.

But the story didn't end there. Not long afterwards, Strelka gave birth to six healthy puppies! And both dogs went on to live long and happy lives.

SPACE DOG GIVES BIRTH TO HEALTHY PUPPIES!

STRELKA'S PUPPIES PROVE SPACEFLIGHT IS NOT HARMFUL

PUSHINKA FOR PRESIDENT!

SPACE DOG PUP PUSHINKA GIVEN TO JOHN F. KENNEDY, PRESIDENT OF THE UNITED STATES OF AMERICA

Oleg was very proud of his two little cosmonauts, for without them one of the most wondrous missions of all might never have taken place!

Belka and Strelka's brave adventure had blazed a trail for humans to follow. Which just goes to show that it doesn't matter where you come from: if two little dogs from the streets of Moscow can make history, then perhaps you can too!

WORLD NEW

NO: 27,356

THE BESTSELLING NEWSPAPER

TODAY'S

DOGS PAVE THE WAY FOR FIRST SPACEMAN

On 12 April 1961, people all over the world listened in amazement to news of the first man in space!

THE SPACE RACE

In 1960, the year Belka and Strelka successfully orbited Earth, the United States and the Soviet Union were in the middle of a Space Race to see who could push the boundaries of space exploration the furthest.

1947

In the 1940s, both nations were working to send animals on missions to space. In 1947, American scientists launched the first living creatures in space – fruit flies.

1949

Then, in 1949, they sent up a monkey called Albert II. Unfortunately he did not survive the mission.

SPACE EXPLORATION TODAY

By the mid 1970s the Space Race had fizzled out, and in recent years scientists from all around the world have worked together on missions to space.

1963

In 1963, French scientists launched the first and only cat ever to be sent to space. Her name was Félicette.

WHERE EXACTLY IS SPACE?

100 km above the Earth there is an invisible line called the Kármán Line. Anything crossing this line is officially in space.

1951

Between 1951–1965, Soviet scientists launched more than 50 dogs. They had to be small enough to fit into a spacecraft, weigh between 6–7 kg and measure no more than 35.5 cm in height.

1960

On board Belka and Strelka's flight in 1960 there were a range of living things, including 40 mice, a rabbit, two white rats, insects and plants.

THE JOURNEY TO SPACE

Belka and Strelka orbit the Earth
(*Sputnik 5*)

First man in space,
Yuri Gagarin (*Vostok 1*)

First woman in space,
Valentina Tereshkova (*Vostok 6*)

Lunar rover, known as
'Moon Buggy', driven on
the Moon (*Apollo 15*)

First men on the Moon, Neil Armstrong,
Michael Collins and Buzz Aldrin (*Apollo 11*)

1963

1961

1969

1971

1960

First British astronaut, Helen Sharman (Project Juno)

Building begins on the International Space Station. There are always six astronauts, who come from all over the world, living on board the ISS

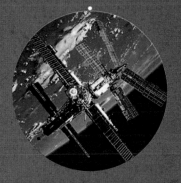

First British ESA (European Space Agency) Astronaut, Tim Peake (Expedition 46/47)

First permanently manned space station built (Mir)

First human on Mars . . . IT COULD BE YOU!

1986

1991

1998

2015

The Future

For all the aspiring explorers, inventors
and dreamers – you are the future – V.S.

For David Bowie – I.D.

First published in Great Britain in 2018 by
Wren & Rook
This edition published in 2019 by Wren & Rook

Text copyright © Hodder & Stoughton Limited, 2018
Illustration copyright © Iris Deppe, 2018
All rights reserved.

ISBN: 978 1 5263 6070 0
E-book ISBN: 978 1 5263 6094 6
10 9 8 7 6 5 4 3 2 1

MIX
Paper from
responsible sources
FSC® C104740

Wren & Rook
An imprint of Hachette Children's Group
Part of Hodder & Stoughton
Carmelite House
50 Victoria Embankment
London EC4Y 0DZ
An Hachette UK Company
www.hachette.co.uk
www.hachettechildrens.co.uk

Publishing Director: Debbie Foy
Senior Editor: Alice Horrocks
Art Director: Laura Hambleton
Designer: Barbara Sido
Printed in China

Every effort has been made to clear copyright.
Should there be any inadvertent omission, please
apply to the publisher for rectification.

The website addresses (URLs) included in this
book were valid at the time of going to press.
However, it is possible that contents or
addresses may have changed since the
publication of this book. No responsibility
for any such changes can be accepted by
either the author or the publisher.

The publisher would like to thank the following
for permission to reproduce their pictures:
Sputnik, 30-31; NASA, 30-31.